Clearing

Winter 1979

Other books by Wendell Berry

Fiction
Nathan Coulter
A Place on Earth
The Memory of Old Jack

Poetry
The Broken Ground
Openings
Findings
Farming: A Hand Book
The Country of Marriage

Essays
The Long-Legged House
A Continuous Harmony
The Hidden Wound
The Unforeseen Wilderness

Wendell Berry

CLEARING

Harcourt Brace Jovanovich
New York and London

Printed in the United States of America

"The Clearing" appeared originally in *The Hudson Review;* other poems appeared first in *Apple, Kayak, Not Man Apart,* and *The Virginia Quarterly Review.*

Library of Congress Cataloging in Publication Data

Berry, Wendell, 1934-
Clearing.
I. Title.
PS3552.E75C55   811'.5'4   76-27422
ISBN 0-15-118150-0
      0-15-618051-0 (pbk.)

A B C D E F G H I J

For Dan Wickenden

Contents

What has been spoiled through man's fault can be made good again through man's work.

I Ching

Handles are shining where my life has passed.
My fields and walls are aching
in my shoulders. My subjects are my objects:
house, barn, beast, hill, and tree.
Reader, make no mistake. The meanings
of these must balance against their weight.

History

For Wallace Stegner

1.
The crops were made. The leaves
were down. Three frosts had lain
upon the broad stone
step beneath the door.
As I walked away
the houses were shut, quiet
under their drifting smokes,
the women stooped at the hearths.
Beyond the farthest tracks
of any domestic beast
my way led me, and into
a place for which I knew
no names. I went by paths
that bespoke intelligence
and memory I did not know.
Noonday held sounds of moving
water, moving air,
enormous stillness
of trees. Though I was weary,
song was near me then,
wordless and gay as a deer
lightly stepping. Learning
the landmarks and the ways
of that land, so I might
go back, if I wanted to,

my mind grew new, and lost
the backward way. I stood
at last, long hunter and child,
where this valley opened,
a word I seemed to know
though I had not heard it.
Behind me, along the crooks
and slants of my approach,
a low song sang itself,
as patient as the light.
On the valley floor the woods
grew rich: great poplars,
beeches, sycamores,
walnuts, sweet gums, lindens,
oaks. They stood apart
and open, the winter light
at rest among them. Yes,
and as I came down
I heard a little stream
pouring into the river.

2.
Since then I have arrived here
many times. I have come
on foot, on horseback, by boat,
and by machine—by earth,
water, air, and fire.
I came with axe and rifle.
I came with a sharp eye
and the price of land. I came

4

in bondage, and I came
in freedom unworth the name.
From the high outlook
of that first day I have come
down two hundred years
across the worked and wasted
slopes, by eroding tracks
of the joyless horsepower of greed.
Through my history's despite
and ruin, I have come
to its remainder, and here
have made the beginning
of a farm intended to become
my art of being here.
By it I would instruct
my wants: they should belong
to each other and to this place.
Until my song comes here
to learn its words, my art
is but the hope of song.

3.
All the lives this place
has had, I have. I eat
my history day by day.
Bird, butterfly, and flower
pass through the seasons of
my flesh. I dine and thrive
on offal and old stone,
and am combined within

the story of the ground.
By this earth's life, I have
its greed and innocence,
its violence, its peace.
Now let me feed my song
upon the life that is here
that is the life that is gone.
This blood has turned to dust
and liquefied again in stem
and vein ten thousand times.
Let what is in the flesh,
O Muse, be brought to mind.

Where

1.
At first there was the woods
that the land lay hidden under,
storing the slow increase
of leaf-fall, flaking bone.
The Indians divided it
only by journeys passing
in silence under the branches.

And then a survey by Thomas
and Walker Daniels: a tract
of a thousand acres lying
in the westward angle
of the meeting of Cane Run
and the Kentucky River.
This sighting of lines passed
among the trees and did not
see them—determination
moving under cover
of the woods like a seducer's hand,
futurity's touch. That was
the coming of geometry,
the possibility of confusion,
and so we come to the record.

For a while even the record
is confused. The first
recorded sellers—never

recorded as buyers—were
"John McEndre & Sarah
his wife," who sold off
ninety-five acres
in 1806 for five shillings,
and in 1817 fifty-four
acres for fifty-four dollars.
This smaller tract, by then,
was the site of a landing
and warehouse known as Sullinger's.
The fifty-four-acre tract
is the one whose history
we follow now. The McEndres
sold it to James Johnston.
And then there is a gap
in the record. The land
came somehow to be owned
by Thomas Smith, upon
whose death in 1865
it was sold to Asa Batts.

Asa Batts kept it
for only six years
and in 1871 sold it
—Sullinger's landing had now
become Lanes Landing—
to A. J. & Matilda Jones,
who divided it into two tracts
of about ten and about
forty acres each.

*

The mind still hungers
for its earth, its bounded
and open space, the term
of its final assent. It keeps
the vision of an independent
modest abundance. It dreams
of cellar and pantry filled,
the source well husbanded.
And yet it learns care
reluctantly, and late.
It suffers plaintively from
its obligations. Long
attention to detail
is a cross it bears only
by congratulating itself.
It would like to hurry up
and get more than it needs
of several pleasant things.
It dreads all the labors
of common decency.
It recalls, with disquieting
sympathy, the motto
of a locally renowned
and long dead kinsman: "Never
set up when you can lay down."

*

The land bears the scars
of minds whose history

was submerged in numbers,
imprinted by no example
of a forebearing mind, corrected,
beloved. A mind cast loose
in whim and greed makes
nature its mirror, and the garden
falls with the man. Great trees
once crowded this bottomland,
so thick that when they were felled
a boy could walk a mile
along their trunks and never
set foot to ground. Where
that forest stood, the fields
grew fine crops of hay:
men tied the timothy heads
together across their horses'
withers; the mountains upstream
were wooded then, and the river
in flood renewed its fields
like the Nile. Given
a live, native tradition
of husbanding and taking care,
that abundance might
have lasted. It did not.
One lifetime of our history
ruined it. The slopes
of the watershed were stripped
of trees. The black topsoil
washed away in the tracks
of logger and plowman.
The creeks, which once ran clear

after the heaviest rains,
ran muddy, dried in summer.
From year to year watching
from his porch, my grandfather
saw a barn roof slowly
rise into sight above
a neighboring ridge as the plows
and rains wore down the hill.
This little has been remembered.
For the rest, one must go
and ponder in the silence
of documents, or decipher
on the land itself the healed
gullies and the unhealed,
the careless furrows drawn
over slopes too steep to plow
where the scrub growth
stands in vision's failure now.

*

Such a mind is as much
a predicament as such
a place. And yet a knowledge
is here that tenses the throat
as for song: the inheritance
of the ones, alive or once
alive, who stand behind
the ones I have imagined,
who took into their minds
the troubles of this place,
blights of love and race,

but saw a good fate here
and willingly paid its cost,
kept it the best they could,
thought of its good,
and mourned the good they lost.

*

The tract of fifty-four
acres first sold in 1817
by John and Sarah McEndre
has this peculiarity:
from then until now, no parent
has ever left it to a child.
Only one man kept it
until he died, only
one of its owners became
its own. John R. Tingle
bought the forty-acre tract
in 1904, and farmed it
nearly half a century,
making the place pay
for itself, living from it,
caring for it, dying
at last "with a little
something put away."
He had no child of his own.
Still known to living men
as "John R." or "Uncle John,"
he was a decent man
by all reports, and his hillside
shows it. Where the bushes

have sheltered it since his time
there are no gullies; the slope's
face is unmarred beneath
the returning woods. Among
the trees we still find
the careful piles of stones
he carried out of his fields.
Under the eaves, his whitewash
still flakes the barn.
The barn was flagstoned where
he stalled his team; the bank
above it was stone-walled.
In spring he followed crops
and beasts to the fields,
and before winter brought
them to the barn. He kept
his place, milked and fed,
waked and slept, helped
his neighbors, imposed on none,
was tolerably satisfied,
and died. And now as I
daily step where his steps
beat upon the ground
the passing of his days
and times, rounds of crops
and seasons, he comes on
into my time. He becomes
one of my reasons, who kept
those rhythms in mind so long.
Men who tread them day
after day, despite complaint

and pain and growing old,
are drawing near to song.

He thinks of the ones before him farming the land then pain + old age. It keeps him going when things get tough.

3.
And to the place that bore
John R. Tingle's name,
came a "developer," foreign
everywhere he went,
his mind a disordered city
with poison in the air.
He *was* that ruinous city
that lives by using up
what ought to last forever.
He was its blind-groping root.
Where Uncle John had walked
behind his team, this man's
mind ran, in haste and fever,
upon the scent of cash,
and destruction followed. When
he came here, he came
to no place he knew or saw,
and by his ignorance
he ruined all he touched.
Like a heavy beast, crazed
or merely stupid, he wallowed
the field he hoped to graze.

*

But condemn the act
and not the man. His effect

is what must be opposed
or corrected. Let
my hands find their work
—now there is no choice—
in what is spoiled, and let
my mouth find better words.

*

There is a way to live
in face of ignorance and greed.
The way is the way of water,
that patiently stays and fills
the place it comes to, until
a way is found. We stayed
three years while the greed
in that man's mind became
the cancer of his dream.
And then we bought from him
the ruin of what once was
the life of plants and beasts
and men. We paid his price,
and saw the last of him.
That night it seemed to me
old John R.'s ghost walked
his fields again, set free,
and in the woods some Indian
spirit stirred, a light
almost dark among the trees.
Again we had signed our names,
this time to a price and labor
nobody else would pay.

It is the price of vision
that we owe, the cost
of what has been here, what
can be. By this we are lost
to other possibility. In fear
and hope, by work and sleep
we are married here.

The Clearing

For Hayden Carruth

1.
Through elm, buckeye, thorn,
box elder, redbud, whitehaw,
locust thicket, all trees
that follow man's neglect,
through snarls and veils
of honeysuckle, tangles
of grape and bittersweet,
sing, chainsaw, the hard song
of vision cutting in.

2.
Vision must have severity
at its edge:

             against neglect,
bushes grown over the pastures,
vines riding down
the fences, the cistern broken;

against the false vision
of the farm dismembered,
sold in pieces on the condition
of the buyer's ignorance,
a disorderly town

of "houses in the country"
inhabited by strangers;

against indifference, the tracks
of the bulldozer running
to gulleys;

       against weariness,
the dread of too much to do,
the wish to make desire
easy, the thought of rest.

3.
"We don't bother nobody,
and we don't want nobody
to bother us," the old woman
declared fiercely
over the fence. She stood
in strange paradise:
a shack built in the blast
of sun on the river bank,
a place under threat of flood,
bought ignorantly, not
to be bothered. And that
is what has come of it,
"the frontier spirit," lost
in the cities, returning now
to be lost in the country,
obscure desire floating
like a cloud upon vision.

22

To be free of labor,
the predicament of other lives,
not to be bothered.

4.
Vision reaches the ground
under sumac and thorn,
under the honeysuckle,
and begins its rise.
It sees clear pasture,
clover and grass, on the worn
hillside going back
to woods, good cropland
in the bottom gone to weeds.
Through time, labor, the fret
of effort, it sees
cattle on the green slope
adrift in the daily current
of hunger. And vision
moderates the saw blade,
the intelligence
and mercy of that power.
Against nature, nature
will serve well enough
a man who does not ask too much.
We leave the walnut trees,
graces of the ground
flourishing in the air.

5.
A man who does not ask too much
becomes the promise of his land.

His marriage married
to his place, he waits

and does not stray. He takes thought
for the return of the dead

to the ground that they may come
to their last avail,

for the rain
that it stay long in reach of roots,

for roots
that they bind the living

to the dead, for sleep
that it bring breath through the dark,

for love in whose keeping
bloom comes to light.

Singularity made him great
in his sight.

This union makes him small,
a part of what he would keep.

6.

As the vision of labor grows
grows the vision of rest.
Weariness is work's shadow.
Labor is no preparation
but takes life as it goes
and casts upon it
death's shadow, which
enough weariness may welcome.
The body's death rises
over its daily labor,
a tree to rest beneath.
But work clarifies
the vision of rest. In rest
the vision of rest is lost.

*

The farm is the proper destiny,
here now and to come.
Leave the body to die
in its time, in the final dignity
that knows no loss in the fallen
high horse of the bones.

7.

In the predicament of other lives
we become mothers of calves,
teaching them, against nature,
to suck a bucket's valved nipple,
caring for them like life

itself to make them complete
animals, independent
of the tit. Fidelity
reaches through the night
to the triumph of their lives,
bawling in the cold barn before
daylight—to become, eaten,
the triumph of other lives
perhaps not worthy of them,
eaters who will recognize
only their own lives
in their daily meat.

*

But no matter. Life
must be served. Get up,
leave the bed, dress
in the cold room, go under
stars to the barn, come
to the greetings of hunger,
the breath a pale awning
in the dark. Feed
the lives that feed
lives.

*

When one sickens
do not let him die. Hold out
against the simple flesh
that would let its life go
in the cold night. While he lives

a thought belongs to him
that will not rest. And then
accept the relief of death.
Drag the heedless carcass
out of the stall, fling it
in the bushes, let it
lie. Hunger will find it,
the bones divide by stealth,
the black head with its star
drift into the hill.

8.
Streets, guns, machines,
quicker fortunes, quicker deaths
bear down on these
hills whose winter trees
keep like memories
the nests of birds. The arrival
may be complete in my time,
and I will see the end
of names: Tingle and Berry
and Lanes. The history
of lives will end then,
the building and wearing away
of earth and flesh will end,
and the history of numbers
will begin. Then why clear
yet again an old farm
scarred by the lack of sight
that scars our souls?

The struggle is on, no
mistake, and I take
the side of life's history
against the coming of numbers.
Make clear what was overgrown.
Cut the brush, drag it
through sumac and briars, pile it,
clear the old fence rows,
the trash dump, stop
the washes, mend the galls,
fence and sow the fields,
bring cattle back to graze
the slopes, bring crops back
to the bottomland. Here
where the time of rain is kept
take what is half ruined
and make it clear, put it
back in mind.

9.
February. A cloudy day
foretelling spring by its warmth
though snow will follow.
You are at work in the worn field
returning now to thought.
The sorrel mare eager
to the burden, you are dragging
cut brush to the pile,
moving in ancestral motions

of axe-stroke, bending
to log chain and trace, speaking
immemorial bidding and praise
to the mare's fine ears.
And you pause to rest
in the quiet day while the mare's
sweated flanks steam.
You stand in a clearing whose cost
you know in tendon and bone.
A kingfisher utters
his harsh cry, rising
from the leafless river.
Again, again, the old
is newly come.

10.
We pile the brush high,
a pyre of cut trees,
not to burn as the way
once was, but to rot and cover
an old scar of the ground.

The dead elm, its stump
and great trunk too heavy to move,
we give to the riddance of fire.
Two days, two nights
it burns, white ash falling
from it light as snow.

It goes into the air.
What bore the wind
the wind will bear.

11.
An evening comes
when we finish work and go,
stumblers under the folding sky,
the field clear behind us.

Work Song

1. *A Lineage*
By the fall of years I learn how it has been
With Jack Beechum, Mat Feltner, Elton Penn,

And their kind, men made for their fields.
I see them stand their ground, bear their yields,

Swaying in all weathers in their long rows,
In the dance that fleshes desire and then goes

Down with the light. They have gone as they came,
And they go. They go by a kind of will. They claim

In the brevity of their strength an ancient joy.
"Make me know it! Hand it to me, boy!"

2. *A Vision*
If we will have the wisdom to survive,
to stand like slow-growing trees
on a ruined place, renewing, enriching it,
if we will make our seasons welcome here,
asking not too much of earth or heaven,
then a long time after we are dead
the lives our lives prepare will live
here, their houses strongly placed
upon the valley sides, fields and gardens
rich in the windows. The river will run

clear, as we will never know it,
and over it, birdsong like a canopy.
On the levels of the hills will be
green meadows, stock bells in noon shade.
On the steeps where greed and ignorance cut down
the old forest, an old forest will stand,
its rich leaf-fall drifting on its roots.
The veins of forgotten springs will have opened.
Families will be singing in the fields.
In their voices they will hear a music
risen out of the ground. They will take
nothing from the ground they will not return,
whatever the grief at parting. Memory,
native to this valley, will spread over it
like a grove, and memory will grow
into legend, legend into song, song
into sacrament. The abundance of this place,
the songs of its people and its birds,
will be health and wisdom and indwelling
light. This is no paradisal dream.
Its hardship is its possibility.

3. *Passion*
Passion has brought me
to this clearing of the ground,
an ancient passion singing
in my veins, beneath speech,
unheard many years, yet
leading me through cities,
streets, and roads,

gatherings, voices, speech,
and again beyond speech,
beyond the words of books,
to stand in this hillside field
in October wind, critical
and solitary, like a horse dumbly
approving of the grass,
the world as clear as light,
as dark as dark.

Can it lead me away
from books? Is it leading me
away? What will I say
to my fellow poets
whose poems I do not read
while this passion keeps me
in the open? What is
this silence coming over me?

I am curious and afraid
one day my poems may pass
through my mind unwritten,
like the freshenings of a stream
in the hills, holding the light
only while they pass, shaping
only what they pass through,
source and destination
the same. I am afraid,
some days, that only vanity
keeps me at my words.

Some days I wait here
empty as a tree
whose birds and leaves
have gone. And I know my words
have gone in search of things.
They are hunting the song
that will celebrate the absence
of what does not belong.

4. *Forsaking All Others*
Because desire and will are strong
I have believed in miraculous deliverances.
I have believed that I would never
have to forsake anything. I have believed
that even at last the strange
woman whose lips drop as a honeycomb
would beckon from her door, and even
in my hurry to reach home her song
would draw me out of my way.
And in spite of reason and belief, even
desire, I have heard a voice saying
that I shall labor here a while, comfort
denied, and then come to a distant place,
a beautiful city or a gentle garden
preserved by someone else's servitude,
where I would take my ease and meditate
the long incoming surf of days.

*

It is not to be. It is not to be.
That is the burden that roughens
my song. That is my joy's burden.
This steep, half-ruined, lovely place,
this graced and wearing labor
longer than my life, this marriage,
blessed and difficult—these have
a partial radiance that is all my light.

5. *A Beginning*
October's completing light falls
on the unfinished patterns of my year.
The sun is yellow in a smudge
of public lies we no longer try
to believe. Speech finally drives us
to silence. Power has weakened us.
Comfort wakens us in fear. We are
a people who must decline or perish.
I have let my mind at last bend down
where human vision begins its rise
in the dark of seeds, wombs of beasts.
It has carried my hands to roots
and foundings, to the mute urging
that in human care clears the field
and turns it green. It reaches
the silence at the tongue's root
in which speech begins. In early mist
I walk in these re-opening fields
as in a forefather's dream. In dream
and sweat the fields have seasoning.

I work to renew a ruined place
that no life be hostage of my comfort.
Let my words then begin in labor.
Let me sing a work song
and an earth song. Let the song of light
fall upon me as it may.
The end of this is not in sight.
And I come to the waning of the year
weary, the way long.

6. *Returning to the Beloved*
The low songs of summer's end
Dreaming in the air, and the light clear,
I drive loads of manure to the field
To make pasture for the coming year.

There is a kind of labor that is absence
In the hurry and fret of growth,
The worry of obligation, time and money,
The threat of summer storm or drouth.

And now we make this return, the team
And I. In the glimmering atmosphere of song
We come and go again, rebuilding promise
In the ground. It will not be long

Before the cold will drive us in. But this, now,
Is where I ought to be, and want to be,
And where I am. Desire and circumstance
Are one. Like a woman's arms this work holds me.

The Bed

1.
Crumbs of rotten stone,
shards of bone, the leavings
and the ruins of lives—
the ground's a grave, and so
it thrives. Another day,
another day, sing
the sleepers in their bed.
Under the bitter ice,
among the overthrown are hid
the seeds, in whose dark
the future and the past
internested lie,
two lovers in their sleep.
A thousand thousand years
will bloom here in the spring,
upon the living sing
the blessing of the dead.

2.
    As though I stood, unaware,
on a great bed, and one of the sleepers
turned, making the footing
uneasy, I see them:
a party of hunters by a low fire,
two men and a boy:
a third man, wounded, lies still,

his body already given
to what is beyond the light.
His eyes follow the movements
of the other men, and rest again
upon the boy. His breaths are loud
in the surrounding quiet.
The fire is cupped in a hollow
of the ground. Behind them
the bluff offers a defense.
They keep their weapons in their hands.

The wounded man cumbering them like a limp,
they have left their pursuers
how far behind they do not know, crossed the river,
climbed here to the valley's rim
to rest, and to ease this death.
Their custom is to bury on these heights.

They speak in sentences I hear the music of
but do not know, and again
are silent in the way of hunters at night,
or in the way of the hunted
who know the ways of the hunters,
listening to what may be coming up
under the wind. Listening
to the distance, they sit in a golden cave
of October leaves, the light
around them restless among the trees.

The man is dead in his stillness
for the time of three breaths

before they notice, or before they move.
Digging with sticks and hands, they scoop
a grave in the valley's lip,
lay him in, cover him, cover earth and rock with leaves,
tramp the fire, spread leaves over the ash
by touch. The place again
is as it was, night filling it.

And they are swiftly on their way,
their steps silent
on the damp leaves. They are gone
as long as the fate of men is
to be gone from the places they have been.

The leaves of the years
fall, and the rains.
Burrow, frost, and root thrust
in the mold. Gravity
gathers the occasions
of an implacable healing.
The dead one has turned
to the light again,
the valley wider by his body's width.

3.
Like the fields, my mind's a bed.
Graves open in my head.

The dead rise and walk about
The timeless fields of thought.

I am by right of birth their own.
I mark like briefly lettered stone

Their beds, and I sing
Their powerful sleep, the opening

By which, nameless or named, they must
Empower and stir again this dust.

To sorrow, their death is long.
Their coming again is song.

From the Crest

1.
What we leave behind to sleep
is ahead of us when we wake.
Cleared, the field must be
kept clear. There are more
clarities to make.
The farm is an infinite form.
Thinking of what may come,
I wake up in the night
and cannot go back to sleep.
The future swells in the dark,
too large a room for one
man to sleep well in.
I think of the work at hand.
Before spring comes again
there is another pasture
to clear and sow, for an end
I desire but cannot know.
Now in the silent keep
of stars and of my work
I lay me down to sleep.

2.
The deepest sleep holds us
to something immutable.
We have fallen
into place, and harmony

surrounds us. We are carried
in the world, in the company
of stars. But as the dawn
approaches, I feel shaping
in my belly, for another day,
my hunger, harder than bone,
keener than fire, and I weave
round it again the kindling
tapestry of desire.

3.

    My life's wave is at its crest.
The thought of work becomes
a friend of the thought of rest.
I see how little avail
one man is, and yet I would not
be a man sitting still,
no little song of desire
traveling the mind's dark woods.

    I am trying to teach my mind
to bear the long, slow growth
of the fields, and to sing
of its passing while it waits.

    The farm must be made a form,
endlessly bringing together
heaven and earth, light
and rain building, dissolving,

building back again
the shapes and actions of the ground.

If it is to be done,
not of the body, not of the will
the strength will come,
but of delight that moves
lovers in their loves,
that moves the sun and stars,
that stirs the leaf, and lifts
the hawk in flight.

From the crest of the wave
the grave is in sight,
the soul's last deep track
in the known. Past there
it gives up roof and fire,
board, bed, and word.
It returns to the wild,
where nothing is done by hand.

I am trying to teach
my mind to accept the finish
that all good work must have:
of hands touching me,
days and weathers passing
over me, the smooth of love,
the wearing of the earth.
At the final stroke
I will be a finished man.

4.

Little farm, motherland,
made, like an abused wife,
by what has nearly been your ruin,
when I speak to you, I speak
to myself, for we are one
body. When I speak to you,
I speak to wife, daughter, son,
whom you have fleshed in your flesh.
And speaking to you, I speak
to all that brotherhood that rises
daily in your substance
and walks, burrows, flies, stands:
plants and beasts whose lives
loop like dolphins through your sod.

5.

Going into the city, coming
home again, I keep you
always in my mind.
Who knows me who does not
know you? The crowds of the streets
do not know that you
are passing among them with me.
They think I am simply a man,
made of a job and clothes
and education. They do not
see who is with me,
or know the resurrection
by which we have come

from the dead. In the city
we must be seemly and quiet
as becomes those who travel
among strangers. But do not
on that account believe
that I am ashamed
to acknowledge you, my friend.
We will write them a poem
to tell them of the great
fellowship, the mystic order,
to which both of us belong.

6.

When I think of death I see
that you are but a passing thought
poised upon the ground,
held in place
by vision, love, and work,
all as passing as a thought.

7.

Beginning and end
thread these fields like a net.
Nosing and shouldering,
the field mouse pats
his anxious routes through the grass,
the mole his cool ones
among the roots; the air
is tensely woven of bird flight,

fluttery at night with bats;
the mind of the honeybee
is the map of bloom.
Like a man, the farm is headed
for the woods. The wild
is already veined in it
everywhere, its thriving.
To love these things one did not
intend is to be a friend
to the beginning and the end.

8.
And when we speak together,
love, our words rise
like leaves, out of our fallen
words. What we have said
becomes an earth we live on
like two trees, whose sheddings
enrich each other, making
both the source of each.

*

When we love, the green
stalks and downturned bells
of lilies grow from our flesh.
Dreams and visions flower
from these beds our bodies are.

9.

The farm travels in snow,
a little world flying
through the Milky Way.
The flakes all fall
into place. But already
the mind begins to shift
its light, clearing space
to receive anew the old fate
of spring. In all the fields
and woods, old work calls
to new. The dead and living
prepare again to mate.

10.

Let the great song come
that sways the branches, that weaves
the nest of the vireo,
that the ground squirrel dreams
in his deep sleep, and wakes,
that the fish hear, that pipes
the minnows over
the shoals. In snow I wait
and sing of the braided
song I only partly hear.
Even in the rising year,
even in the spring,
the little can hope to sing
only in praise of the great.

Reverdure

1.
You never know
what you are going to learn.

2.
The wintering mind turns
inward, like the earth
wintering. Beneath frost
it keeps future and past
alive. In spring it rises
from its deeps, folds out
again to light. Mind
and leaf unflex in shine.

3.
How to get in
and out of your mind?
The way in prepares
the way out.

The groundhog, who turned
his tail to the cold, now
sticks out his face.

4.
In the first warm morning
the black calf walks down
to the river, the light irised

in his hair. Over his back
leap the shadows of willows
leafing. The good sun
makes him go easy.

5.
The phoebes have come back.

The drums of the woodpeckers
ask and answer.

The blue of the bluebird
is in the leafless apple tree,
new breath.

The redbird sings
O let it come, O

let it, let it.

6.
An old grandmother
a little surprised
to be waking up again,
the ground slowly remembers
the shapes of grassblades,
stems, leaves, birds,
cattle, people, songs.

7.

The slope whose scars I mended
turns green now.
Healing becomes health.
Reverdure is my calling.

8.

One thing work gives
is the joy of not working,
a minute here or there
when I stand and only breathe,
receiving the good of the air.
It comes back. Good work done
comes back into the mind,
a free breath drawn.

9.

Though I came here
by history's ruin, reverdure
is my calling:
to make these scars grow grass.
I survive this fate and labor
by fascination.

10.

I want to fence the thicket-ridden field
unused all my life, and turn in the calves
to browse the vines and leaves in May.
They will begin to open it, eating
the low growth, letting vision find its way
in among the close-standing trunks.

And then in the winters, as I need,
I will thin the trees, leaving the walnuts,
poplars, ashes, oaks, burning
what I cut to heat the house. Springs,
on the frozen mornings of early March,
I will sow the opened land. Slowly
good pasture will widen over the slope
in the shade of scattered tall trees,
change doing the ground no harm.

11.
And so, in the first warmth of the year,
I went up with saw and axe
to cut a way in. I made a road, I made
a thought-way under the trees, up
the slope, and that was ancient work.
In rhyme of flesh with flesh, time
with time, act with act, I made my way
into the woods, leaving an order
that was mine, a way opening behind me
by which I came out again.

12.
Above that thicket growth
the hillside steepens,
the trees are old. The farm
reaches one of its limits
there, and finds its example.
No leaf falls there that is lost;
all that falls rises, opens,
sings; what was, is.

And this steep woods will be
left standing, a part
of the farm not farmed,
its sacred grove, where we
will have nothing to do.
The trees live in eternity
and they live now. Their roots
are in life and death.
They have the earthly health
whose signature is song.

13.
And there are ways
the deer walk in darkness
that are clear.
It is not by will
I know this,
but by willingness,
by being here.

14.
It is time again I made an end to words
for a while—for this time,
or for all time. Any end may last.
I love this warm light room, where words
have kept me through the cold days.
But now song surrounds it, the fields
around it are green, and I must turn away
from books, put past and future behind,
to come into the presence of this time.

Sort of has Native American quality to it wf. to song